15-Minute Foodie

Colorful Foods in 15 Minutes or Less

by Tamara JM Peterson

CAPSTONE PRESS
a capstone imprint

Dabble Lab is published by Capstone Press, an imprint of Capstone.
1710 Roe Crest Drive, North Mankato, Minnesota 56003
capstonepub.com

Copyright © 2024 by Capstone. All rights reserved. No part of this publication may be reproduced in whole or in part, or stored in a retrieval system, or transmitted in any form or by any means, electronic, mechanical, photocopying, recording, or otherwise, without written permission of the publisher.

Library of Congress Cataloging-in-Publication Data
Names: Peterson, Tamara JM, author.
Title: Colorful foods in 15 minutes or less / by Tamara JM Peterson.
Description: North Mankato, Minnesota : Capstone Press, a Capstone imprint, [2024] |
Series: 15-minute foodie | Includes bibliographical references. | Audience: Ages 8-11 |
Audience: Grades 4-6 | Summary: "Looking to add a quick burst of color to your meals and snacks? Become a 15-minute foodie! Blend your favorite fruits into a layered rainbow smoothie. Roll up vibrant shrimp and vegetable spring rolls. Serve up a Southwest bowl filled with bright pops of color. These quick, fun, yummy recipes will be ready to enjoy in 15 minutes or less"— Provided by publisher.
Identifiers: LCCN 2023023848 (print) | LCCN 2023023849 (ebook) |
ISBN 9781669061533 (hardcover) | ISBN 9781669061496 (pdf) |
ISBN 9781669061519 (kindle edition) | ISBN 9781669061502 (epub)
Subjects: LCSH: Quick and easy cooking—Juvenile literature.
Classification: LCC TX652.5 .P49 2024 (print) | LCC TX652.5 (ebook) |
DDC 641.5/123—dc23/eng/20230524
LC record available at https://lccn.loc.gov/2023023848
LC ebook record available at https://lccn.loc.gov/2023023849

Image Credits
Adobe Stock: ksena32, 30, 31 (cherries), xamtiw, 7 (granola); iStockphoto: andresr, 4, baibaz, Front Cover (fruit), VioletaStoimenova, 5; Mighty Media, Inc.: project photos; Shutterstock: Brent Hofacker, 9 (lime), ifong, 29, Yuriy Bogatirev, 7 (kiwi)

Design Elements
iStockphoto: Sirintra_Pumsopa, yugoro; Mighty Media, Inc.

Editorial Credits
Editor: Jessica Rusick
Designers: Sarah DeYoung and Denise Hamernik
Cooks: Tamara JM Peterson and Chelsey Luciow

All internet sites appearing in back matter were available and accurate when this book was sent to press.

The publisher and the author shall not be liable for any damages allegedly arising from the information in this book, and they specifically disclaim any liability from the use or application of any of the contents of this book.

Printed and bound in China. 5593

Table of Contents

Colorful Foods in Fifteen! 4

Yogurt Sunrise 6

Honey Lime Fruit Salad. 8

Rainbow Pancakes 10

Super Colorful Stir-Fry 12

Chicken Salad Wrap 14

Rainbow Baguette 16

Veggie Pinwheels 18

Spring Rolls 20

Southwest Pepper Bowl 22

Rainbow Pizza. 24

Chicken Fajitas 26

Rainbow Smoothie 28

Layered Gelatin Cups. 30

Read More 32

Internet Sites 32

About the Author 32

Colorful Foods in Fifteen!

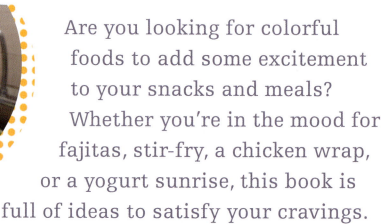

Are you looking for colorful foods to add some excitement to your snacks and meals? Whether you're in the mood for fajitas, stir-fry, a chicken wrap, or a yogurt sunrise, this book is full of ideas to satisfy your cravings. And the best part is, these recipes come together in 15 minutes or less! So grab your kitchen supplies and read through the tips on the next page. Soon enough, you'll be a 15-minute foodie!

Basic Supplies

baking sheet

blender

frying pan

knife and cutting board

large spoon

measuring cups and spoons

mixing bowls

spatula

toothpicks

whisk

zester or grater with small holes

Kitchen Tips

Ask an adult for permission before you make a recipe.

Read through the recipe and set out all ingredients and supplies before you start cooking.

Using metric tools? Use the conversion chart below to make your recipe measure up.

Wash your hands before and after you handle food. Wash and dry fresh produce before use.

Ask an adult for help when using a knife, blender, or stovetop. Wear oven mitts when removing items from the oven or microwave.

When you are done making food, clean your work surface. Wash dirty dishes and put all supplies and ingredients back where you found them.

Standard	Metric
¼ teaspoon	1.25 grams or milliliters
½ teaspoon	2.5 g or mL
1 teaspoon	5 g or mL
1 tablespoon	15 g or mL
¼ cup	57 g (dry) or 60 mL (liquid)
⅓ cup	75 g (dry) or 80 mL (liquid)
½ cup	114 g (dry) or 125 mL (liquid)
⅔ cup	150 g (dry) or 160 mL (liquid)
¾ cup	170 g (dry) or 175 mL (liquid)
1 cup	227 g (dry) or 240 mL (liquid)
1 quart	950 mL

Yogurt Sunrise

Start your day in a colorful way with fresh fruit and yogurt!

Ingredients

1 cup yogurt
  (plain, vanilla, or honey)
¼ cup raspberries
2 strawberries, halved
¼ cup canned mandarin
  orange pieces
¼ cup pineapple chunks
1 kiwi
¼ cup blueberries
granola (optional)

Supplies

knife and cutting board
measuring cups
plate
spatula
paring knife or peeler

1. Spread the yogurt on the plate with the spatula.

2. Arrange a row of raspberries on the top end of the plate. Place a row of strawberries beneath the raspberries.

3. Add a row of orange pieces and a row of pineapple beneath the strawberries.

4. Cut the ends off the kiwi. Use the paring knife or peeler to remove the kiwi's skin. Cut the kiwi into rounds. Then cut the rounds into quarters. Place the kiwi pieces in a row beneath the pineapple.

5. Add a row of blueberries to finish the plate.

6. If you'd like, sprinkle granola on top of the fruit and yogurt. Then dig in!

Honey Lime Fruit Salad

Honey lime dressing gives this colorful fruit salad an extra punch of sweetness and tartness.

Ingredients

1 kiwi
½ cup strawberries, halved
½ cup pineapple chunks
½ cup blackberries
½ cup raspberries
½ cup grapes, halved
½ cup canned mandarin orange pieces
½ cup peach chunks
coconut flakes (optional)
1 lime
2 tablespoons honey

Supplies

knife and cutting board
measuring cups and spoons
paring knife or peeler
large bowl
zester or grater with small holes
small bowl
whisk
large spoon
serving bowl

Food Tip

Don't zest the white layer under the lime's green skin. It may make your fruit salad bitter!

1. Cut the ends off the kiwi. Use the paring knife or peeler to remove the kiwi's skin. Cut the kiwi into rounds. Then cut the rounds into quarters.

2. Put all the fruit into the large bowl. Add coconut flakes if you'd like. Use your hands to gently toss the mixture.

3. Lightly zest the green outer skin of the lime. Place the zest in the small bowl. Cut the lime into quarters and squeeze the juice into the small bowl. Remove any seeds.

4. Add the honey to the small bowl. Whisk the mixture to make dressing.

5. Drizzle the dressing over the fruit. Gently stir the mixture together with the spoon.

6. Spoon some of the fruit salad into the serving bowl. Enjoy!

Rainbow Pancakes

Take breakfast up a notch by using fruit to make colorful (and tasty!) pancakes.

Ingredients

1 large egg
1 cup milk
2 tablespoons oil
2 tablespoons sugar
½ teaspoon salt
2 teaspoons baking
  powder
1 cup flour
¼ cup raspberries
¼ cup canned mandarin
  orange pieces
¼ cup pineapple chunks
¼ cup blackberries
food coloring (optional)
1 tablespoon oil or butter,
  plus extra
whipped cream,
  sprinkles, or other
  toppings (optional)

Supplies

knife and cutting board
measuring cups and
  spoons
mixing bowl
whisk
4 plastic storage bags
frying pan
scissors
spatula
plate

1. Whisk together the egg, milk, oil, sugar, salt, baking powder, and flour in the mixing bowl to make batter.

2. Pour one-quarter of the batter into each plastic storage bag.

3. Add the raspberries to one bag and seal it. Carefully squish the bag to mix the raspberries into the batter. If you would like a stronger color, add one drop of coordinating food coloring to the bag.

4. Repeat step 3 to mix the orange, pineapple, and blackberries into the other three bags. Remove any air and tightly seal the bags.

5. Heat the butter or oil in the frying pan over medium heat.

6. Clip a bottom corner from one bag of batter. Squeeze the batter into the frying pan to make a pancake.

7. When the pancake is done bubbling, use the spatula to carefully flip it. Let the pancake cook for another minute. Then transfer it onto the plate.

8. Repeat steps 6 and 7 using the remaining bags of pancake batter. Add more oil or butter to the pan between pancakes if necessary.

9. Top your pancakes with whipped cream, sprinkles, or other toppings of your choice. Then enjoy your colorful breakfast!

Super Colorful Stir-Fry

Use vegetables in an array of colors to make a quick, sizzling stir-fry.

Food Fact! To julienne ingredients means to cut them into thin strips.

Ingredients

1 tablespoon soy sauce
2 tablespoons honey
½ teaspoon sesame oil (optional)
2 tablespoons olive oil
½ cup onion, julienned
½ cup carrots, julienned
1 tablespoon garlic, chopped
1 cup bell peppers, julienned
½ cup celery, sliced
1 tablespoon fresh ginger, chopped (or ½ teaspoon dried ginger)
1 cup cooked chicken, sliced
cooked rice or noodles (optional)

Supplies

knife and cutting board
measuring cups and spoons
small bowl
spoon
frying pan
spatula

1. Mix the soy sauce, honey, and sesame oil in the small bowl. Set the bowl aside.

2. Heat the olive oil in the frying pan on medium high. Add the onion and carrots to the pan and cook for three minutes. Stir the mixture continuously with the spatula.

3. Add the garlic, bell peppers, celery, and ginger. Cook for three more minutes, stirring continuously.

4. Add the chicken to the pan and stir.

5. Pour the soy sauce mixture into the frying pan. Cook the stir-fry for an additional two minutes.

6. Serve the stir-fry with rice or noodles if you'd like. Or enjoy it as is!

Chicken Salad Wrap

On the go? No problem. Just whip up this brightly colored chicken salad wrap and run out the door!

Ingredients

½ cup cooked chicken, chopped
¼ cup carrots, julienned
¼ cup onion, diced
¼ cup bell peppers, diced
¼ cup celery, diced
¼ cup grapes, quartered
¼ cup nuts (optional)
½ cup ranch dressing
1 large flour tortilla
¼ cup shredded lettuce

Supplies

knife and cutting board
measuring cups
large bowl
spoon
2 toothpicks

1. Put the chicken, carrots, onion, bell peppers, celery, grapes, and nuts into the large bowl.

2. Add the ranch dressing to the bowl and stir the mixture.

3. Use the spoon to spread the mixture across the middle of the tortilla.

4. Lay ¼ cup lettuce around the chicken mixture.

5. Carefully but firmly roll the tortilla. Cut the wrap down the middle.

6. Poke one toothpick into the center of each half to hold them together. Remove the toothpicks when you're ready to dig in!

Rainbow Baguette

Mix and match flavors and colors with this fun, simple appetizer.

Ingredients

1 baguette
hummus, sunflower butter, or nut butter
¼ cup yam, sliced
¼ cup yellow squash, sliced
¼ cup eggplant, sliced
1½ tablespoons olive oil
½ teaspoon sage
½ teaspoon thyme
½ teaspoon oregano
1 avocado
½ teaspoon cilantro leaves
¼ cup blueberries
¼ cup raspberries

Supplies

knife and cutting board
measuring cups and spoons
spreading knife
small bowl
microwave-safe plate
2 serving plates

1. Slice the baguette into 12 even rounds. Spread hummus, sunflower butter, or nut butter on each baguette round.

2. Toss the yam, squash, and eggplant slices with 1 tablespoon olive oil in the small bowl.

3. Lay the yam, squash, and eggplant on the microwave-safe plate. Sprinkle sage on the yam, thyme on the squash, and oregano on the eggplant. Microwave the plate for two minutes.

4. Cut the avocado in half and remove the pit. Cut the flesh into thin slices while it's still in the peel. Then scoop the slices out of the peel and cut them in half.

5. Coat the avocado with ½ tablespoon olive oil. Set several slices on two baguette rounds. Lay cilantro leaves on top.

6. Top two baguette rounds with blueberries and two with raspberries. Place the yam, squash, and eggplant on the remaining baguette rounds.

7. Serve up one of each baguette flavor per plate!

Veggie Pinwheels

Need a fun party dish in a hurry?
Give these pinwheels a spin.

Ingredients

½ cup cream cheese
1 tablespoon ranch dressing
½ cup red bell pepper, julienned
½ cup carrots, julienned
½ cup yellow bell pepper, julienned
½ cup baby spinach leaves
½ cup shredded purple cabbage
4 large flour tortillas

Supplies

knife and cutting board
measuring cups and spoons
small bowl
spoon
spatula
toothpicks (optional)

1. Combine the cream cheese and ranch dressing in the small bowl. Stir well.

2. Spread one-quarter of the cream cheese and ranch mixture on each tortilla with the spatula.

3. Lay the red bell pepper, carrots, yellow bell pepper, baby spinach, and purple cabbage on each tortilla in stripes. Leave about one-third of each tortilla uncovered. This will help the pinwheel stay rolled.

4. Carefully but firmly roll each tortilla, starting at the end with the red bell pepper. If you'd like, add six toothpicks along each tortilla to help the roll stay together.

5. Cut each roll in half. Cut each half into thirds to make six pinwheels per tortilla.

6. Serve the pinwheels for lunch or at a party!

Spring Rolls

These spring rolls make a fun and tasty snack. The translucent wrappers allow you to see all the colors inside!

Food Fact!
Many spring roll wrappers are made with rice flour and water.

Ingredients

6 spring roll wrappers
16 precooked shrimp
1 teaspoon olive oil
¼ cup red bell pepper, julienned
¼ cup yellow bell pepper, julienned
¼ cup cucumber, julienned
2 green onions, chopped
¼ cup shredded purple cabbage
1 tablespoon creamy peanut butter
1 teaspoon sesame oil
1 teaspoon lime juice
1 teaspoon rice vinegar
¼ teaspoon garlic powder

Supplies

knife and cutting board
measuring cups and spoons
plate
water
small bowl
small whisk or fork
chopsticks (optional)

1. Spread the olive oil on the plate with your fingers. It will prevent the spring roll wrappers from sticking to the plate.

2. Run a spring roll wrapper under water and set it on the oiled plate.

3. Place four shrimp along the edge of the wrapper. Place the red bell pepper, yellow bell pepper, cucumber, green onions, and cabbage next to the shrimp in stripes.

4. Fold the sides of the wrapper in. Carefully but firmly roll the wrapper, starting from the shrimp side.

5. Repeat steps 2 through 4 to make more spring rolls.

6. In the small bowl, combine the peanut butter, sesame oil, lime juice, rice vinegar, and garlic powder to make dipping sauce. Use the small whisk or fork to mix well.

7. Cut the spring rolls in half to serve. If you'd like, use chopsticks to dip the spring rolls!

Southwest Pepper Bowl

This hearty bowl makes the perfect healthy meal. Bell peppers, corn, and green onion also give it pops of color!

Ingredients

¼ cup quick-cooking quinoa
1 cup water
2 tablespoons olive oil
½ cup bell peppers, chopped
½ cup green onion, chopped
½ cup corn
½ cup pinto or black beans
1 teaspoon cumin
½ cup salsa
shredded cheese (optional)
cilantro (optional)
tortilla chips

Supplies

knife and cutting board
measuring cups and spoons
microwave-safe bowl
microwave-safe plate
spoon
frying pan

1. Mix the quinoa and water in the microwave-safe bowl. Cover the bowl with the plate and microwave it for six minutes. Check periodically to make sure the water does not boil over.

2. Remove the plate from the bowl and stir the quinoa. Replace the plate and microwave for four more minutes. Let the quinoa cool.

3. While the quinoa cools, heat the olive oil in the frying pan on high. Add the bell peppers and green onion and cook for two minutes.

4. Add the corn, beans, cumin, and salsa to the pan. Mix well and cook for two minutes.

5. Add the quinoa to the pan and stir.

6. Your Southwest bowl is ready to serve! If you'd like, top it with shredded cheese and cilantro. Serve tortilla chips on the side!

Rainbow Pizza

Pizza is the perfect food to share! This healthy, colorful pizza will be the star of any pizza party.

Ingredients

1 tablespoon olive oil
¼ cup sun-dried tomatoes, chopped
¼ cup orange bell pepper, chopped
¼ cup broccoli, chopped
¼ cup corn
½ tablespoon garlic, minced
flatbread
marinara sauce
mozzarella cheese

Supplies

knife and cutting board
measuring cups and spoons
frying pan
spatula
baking sheet

1. Preheat the oven to 350 degrees Fahrenheit (177 degrees Celsius).

2. Heat the olive oil in the frying pan on high. Add the sun-dried tomatoes, bell pepper, broccoli, corn, and garlic. Cook for five minutes, stirring occasionally.

3. While the vegetables cook, spread marinara sauce over the flatbread. Cover the marinara with a layer of mozzarella cheese.

4. Arrange the tomatoes, bell pepper, corn, and broccoli across the pizza.

5. Place the pizza on the baking sheet. Bake for five minutes or until the cheese is bubbly.

6. Remove the pizza from the oven and let it cool. Enjoy!

Chicken Fajitas

A fiesta is even better with fajitas!
These colorful fajitas are sure to be delicious.

Ingredients

2 tablespoons cilantro, chopped (or 1 teaspoon dried cilantro)
¼ cup sour cream
1 tablespoon lime juice
½ teaspoon salt
½ teaspoon pepper
3 tablespoons olive oil
1½ tablespoons garlic, minced
¼ cup onion, julienned
1 cup bell peppers, julienned
1 cup cooked chicken
½ teaspoon cumin
½ teaspoon chili powder
½ teaspoon oregano
1 avocado
4 large flour tortillas
½ cup shredded lettuce
shredded cheese (optional)

Supplies

knife and cutting board
measuring cups and spoons
small bowl
spoon
frying pan
spatula

1. In the small bowl, mix the cilantro, sour cream, lime juice, salt, pepper, 1 tablespoon olive oil, and 1 tablespoon garlic for the dressing. Set aside.

2. Heat the remaining olive oil in the frying pan on high. Add the onion, bell peppers, and remaining garlic. Cook for four minutes, stirring occasionally.

3. Add the chicken, cumin, chili powder, and oregano. Stir well and cook until the chicken is heated through. This is the fajita filling.

4. Cut the avocado in half and remove the pit. Cut the flesh into thin slices while it's still in the peel. Then scoop the slices out.

5. Fill each tortilla with one-quarter of the fajita filling, lettuce, and avocado.

6. Drizzle a spoonful of the dressing over the top of the filling.

7. If you'd like, add shredded cheese to your fajitas. Then dig in!

Rainbow Smoothie

Keep cool on a hot day by slurping up a rainbow through your straw.

Ingredients

Green: 4 spinach leaves, ½ kiwi, ⅓ banana, 1 tablespoon Greek yogurt

Yellow: 4 pineapple chunks, 4 mango chunks, ⅓ banana, 1 tablespoon Greek yogurt

Orange: ⅓ banana, 4 orange pieces, 3 raspberries

Red: 4 raspberries, 4 strawberries, 1 tablespoon pineapple juice

Purple: 6 blueberries, 4 blackberries, 1 tablespoon Greek yogurt

Supplies

knife and cutting board
spoon
measuring spoons
blender
1 tall, clear glass
straw (optional)

1. Cut the kiwi in half. Use the spoon to scoop the flesh of one half out of the peel.

2. Blend the first smoothie color. Pour the smoothie into the glass.

3. Rinse and dry the blender. Blend the next color. Slowly spoon it on top of the smoothie, being careful not to mix it into the color below.

4. Repeat step 3 with the remaining colors.

5. If you'd like, use a straw to sip your delicious rainbow smoothie!

Food Tip

Freeze the glass before making your smoothie. This will help keep the smoothie cool as you blend each color!

Ingredients

3 gelatin cups of different colors
3 cups whipped cream
2 maraschino cherries (optional)

Supplies

spoon
2 tall, clear glasses

1. Spoon half of one gelatin cup into each glass.
2. Add ½ cup whipped cream to each glass.
3. Repeat steps 1 and 2 with the remaining gelatin and whipped cream.
4. If you'd like, top each glass with one cherry. Dig in and enjoy!

Food Fact!

Maraschino cherries are dyed red and preserved in sugar syrup. They are often used to top desserts!

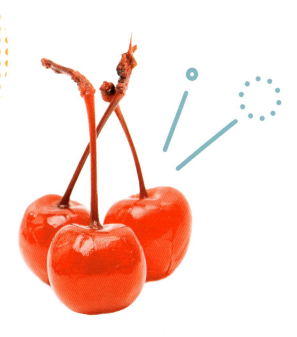

Read More

Atherton, David. *Bake, Make, and Learn to Cook: Fun and Healthy Recipes for Young Cooks*. Somerville, MA: Candlewick Press, 2021.

Hoena, Blake A. *The Bucket List Guide to Food*. North Mankato, MN: Capstone Press, 2023.

Woollard, Rebecca. *The No-Cook Cookbook*. New York: DK Publishing, 2021.

Internet Sites

Easy Recipes That Kids Can Make
foodnetwork.com/recipes/packages/recipes-for-kids/cooking-with-kids/recipes-kids-can-make

Eat a Rainbow
wholekidsfoundation.org/kids-club/eat-a-rainbow

What Makes a Food Super?
wonderopolis.org/wonder/What-Makes-a-Food-Super

About the Author

Tami grew up eating only peanut butter and jelly sandwiches and mac and cheese. It wasn't until she was an adult that food sparked her interest. Since then, she has thrown herself into trying new foods and improving every recipe she can find. She lives in Minnesota with her husband, two daughters, and a big orange cat.